Eight Keys To A Better Me

Text by William J. Briggs, Ed.D.

Illustrations by Lynne Marie Davis

D1158736

Acknowledgements:

We thank the following educators for their participation and advice:

Dr. Shirley M. Fawley, Dr. Elizabeth B. Pitts, Mrs. Jane S. Queen

Special assistance from:

Dr. Jerry Ballard, Merriana Branan, Leslie Underwood

This book belongs to:

Rylan

My name

Randall

My school

My principal

My teacher

DISTRIBUTED EXCLUSIVELY BY

Family Traditions

2936 Rousseau Court
P.O. Box 550968
Gastonia, NC 28055-0968
1-800-548-6615
www.fidelityassociates.com

Purpose of Eight Keys To A Better Me

A Word to Parents and Teachers

Today, more than ever before, the young people of our nation are under attack from highly destructive forces which can disrupt, if not ruin, their lives. As teachers and parents, you are aware of the devastating effect that drugs, child pornography and juvenile crime can have in creating a sense of diminished self-worth and low self-esteem.

A Positive Response

It has been said, "It is better to build children than to repair adults." Therefore, we know you welcome the action of concerned business and professional people who are acting to curb these excesses. This gift book is their way of saying, "We care and we want to help." Teachers and parents can encourage the continuation of this program by expressing their appreciation to those responsible for the gift.

Eight Keys To A Better Me lists and illustrates eight key traits which could influence children in their character development that will lead to a better self-image, to better relationships with others, and to a better life.

We hope that **Eight Keys To A Better Me** will become one of your child's favorite books.

The Publisher

1. HONESTY

is being truthful to myself and to others.

Being honest helps others trust me.
Honesty is: Doing my own work in school.

— Paying for things I want from the store.

— Telling the truth if I do something wrong.

— Returning
something
which does not
belong to me.

2. RESPECT

is giving consideration to and treating others politely.
Showing respect for others shows I respect myself.

— Helping older people
when they need help.

— Listening to my teacher at school.

— Keeping myself
neat and clean.

— Keeping my school
and desk clean.

— Placing litter into trash cans,
  to keep my environment clean.

— Obeying the law and cooperating with the police when they try to help me.

3. PATRIOTISM

is loving my country and devoting myself to its good.

Patriotism shows my love for America.

Pledge of Allegiance

I pledge allegiance to the flag of the United States of America and to the republic for which it stands; one nation, under God, indivisible, with liberty and justice for all.

— Appreciating my country's history.

— Helping my parents get out to vote.

— Appreciating those who protect my country.

4. KINDNESS

is wanting to make others happy.

Kindness makes good feelings.

— Helping someone
who needs my help.

— Taking care of my little brother or sister.

— Feeding my pet.

— Welcoming
new students
to my school.

5. COURAGE

is being brave.

Having courage makes things less scary.
I show courage by: Saying, "No!"

— Learning to accept the dark and scary things.

— Working and
striving for success.

6. RESPONSIBILITY

is doing what I know is right.

— Doing jobs my parents
ask me to do.

— Taking my own pencil and paper to school.

— Being on time.

— Keeping my promise when I say I'll help.

7. FEELINGS

Being aware of myself and others.

I show my feelings by: Showing I care.

— Sharing in another's happiness.

— Knowing it is okay to be afraid when trying something new.

— Sharing my thoughts and emotions with Mom and Dad.

8. SELF WORTH

is feeling good about myself by:

— Being patriotic.

— Being kind.

Keep Going

— Recognizing my feelings.

I, _____,
now hold the Eight Keys To A Better Me.

Paste
your
picture
here

Kindness Patriotism Self-Worth Courage Honesty Feelings Respect Responsibility

What does a "better me" mean?

You know some of the answers. You know some of the ways in which you are different from every other person, but you do not know all the ways.

You will have to think about them. It may take a long, long time. It may even take most of the rest of your life to find some of the answers.

While you are finding answers, remember these **Eight Keys**.

Use the space below to write your thoughts.

_____

_____

_____

_____

_____

_____

_____

_____

_____

_____

_____

_____

_____

_____

_____

Date _____